Poetry is the spo[illegible]
overflow of powerful
feelings; it takes its origin
from emotion recollected
in tranquillity.

– *William Wordsworth.*

Contents

Poetry

Country Calendar

From The Manse Window

Welcome, Spring!

THE first day of spring! So what makes me sure?
The sight of bright daffodils right by my door?
The golden-green catkins that bounce on the breeze,
The blue of the sky or the buds on the trees?
The lambs in the meadows, the larks on the wing,
Are these the glad omens that tell me it's spring?
Well, no. There's a sign that is much more exact –
Today has a something that so far has lacked,
For there on the clothesline my washing hangs high,
And what's more – yes, really – it's nearly all dry!

– Maggie Ingall.

New Beginnings

IN spring nature's rebirth is found everywhere.
In everyday life new beginnings are there,
The commencement of summer, of hot sunny days;
At the rise of a curtain when an orchestra plays.
A marriage, commitment to start a new life,
The thrill of togetherness as man and wife.
The birth of a baby, buying your first home;
Travelling and the chance to explore and to roam.
A child's new beginning at school, playing sport;
Beginning a hobby, a new line of thought.
Rekindling a friendship and loving again,
And the start of good health after suffering pain.
A new opportunity, different career;
Determined and hopeful in every new year.
A day starting badly can suddenly change,
For your positive thoughts can all things rearrange.
A house move, a project, a stranger you've met
Can restore your faith and sad memories forget,
So look for your rainbow which follows the rain,
For it holds every kind of beginning again.

– Chrissy Greenslade.

The First Warm Day

OPEN the windows, let in the sun,
Reach for the duster – spring has begun!
Blow out the cobwebs, mop the hall floor,
Polish the brass upon the front door.
Wash all the curtains and hang them to dry,
Watch them all flap 'neath the cloud-scattered sky.
All through the house vacuum and scrub,
Brushes should sweep and J-cloths should rub.
Clean up the dirty! Clean up the dusty!
Clean up each corner you smell to be musty!
Chase out the winter! Chase out the gloom!
Bring sunlight and sweetness into each room!
Wake your whole house from its long winter doze,
A pleasure for eyes, a delight for the nose.

– Antony Burr.

The Cliff-top

HOW I love this place!
The soothing sound of lapping seas
And gentle stirring of the breeze;
Such soothing sights of promised spring;
Gulls gliding, joyful, on the wing.
On golden gorse I spy a bee,
Alerted, warmed, glad to be free.
How blessed to have this glorious coast!
Tranquillity, the perfect host,
Has welcomed me to share a part
Of this, my place, which owns my heart.

– Chrissy Greenslade.

from the Manse Window

The Gift Of Giving

HAVE you recovered from Christmas yet? Perhaps you are well on your way to making plans for the next! Well, now is the time of year to start thinking of Christmas!

Actually, I was thinking of the charity "Operation Christmas Child", which requires a year-round effort to fill the shoe boxes that are collected from all over the country to send to children in over 15 countries. By Christmas, it plans to have over a million shoe boxes from all around Britain. Perhaps you, or someone you know, will be filling one. Be assured that, by the time you read this, work on this year's gifts will be well underway.

Although the plan is for the boxes to be given as Christmas presents, in reality many of them do not arrive at their destination until the early months of the New Year. So while we are collecting suitable gifts for one year, last year's boxes are still being given out to some of the recipients who live in hard-to-reach places. All the children and families who receive the gift of a shoe box are special, of course, but those who live in some of the world's remotest regions need to know they are not forgotten by those of us in the rest of the world.

As soon as possible in the year, people start knitting or sewing. At our church, some of us formed a craft group early in the year, which brings people together to enjoy each other's company and to exchange ideas. Hats, scarves and gloves provide colour and warmth for those countries where this is needed, and we seem to compete with each other to see who can make them in the brightest colours, making them appealing to the youngest children. Handbags add an air of sophistication to a little girl's wardrobe, and can make them the envy of their friends, and glove puppets are also popular toys. We have to be careful, however, as home-made cuddly toys stuffed by ourselves are often not allowed through International Customs.

Another item that we hope will prove popular for older girls is a little sewing-kit filled with an assortment of needle-cases, scraps of material, threads, lace and ribbons, all topped off with a little bag of buttons.

Our group meets together every few weeks, but in between there

Thinkstockphotos.

By Kathrine Davey, Mansfield Methodist Preacher.

is much frantic activity in people's homes. We contribute what we can, although we all work at different rates and often have to multi-task with many other commitments. In case we find the need for more inspiration, there are also a lot of other ideas from all over the country that are shared on the "Operation Christmas Child" website.

It is not a large church, but everyone seems to be involved in some way. People of all ages develop eagle eyes as we spot all sorts of ideas for suitable gifts. Cuddly toys are always popular and are gathered from various sources – if any suitable ones are seen while out shopping they are quickly snapped up. The parent-and-toddler group is also a good place to garner contributions.

There are many easily available items like pens, pencils and stationery, and toothbrushes, toothpaste and soap are always welcome. Children in many countries need to be able to provide many of their own items for education, or perhaps they like to draw for pleasure, and in many cases the opportunities for personal hygiene are also limited. The things we often consider necessities are thought of as luxuries that are either unaffordable or unavailable by too many people.

AFTER months of knitting, sewing and buying, all the shoe boxes are covered with brightly coloured Christmas wrapping-paper, and then the gifts are chosen to go inside them. We start filling the shoe boxes in September and October, bearing in mind the age of the boy or girl that will receive them. We make sure that all the boxes are as full as they can be, and that they contain something to play with or cuddle, something to write or colour with, a picture book even the youngest will appreciate, something to wash with and something to wear. We also add some sweets.

As the weeks go by, shoe boxes begin to arrive from local churches, schools and groups, as our church is the main collection centre for the area. They are all checked to make sure they contain items from all the above categories and do not contain anything that might be dangerous or upsetting.

The final act for the church is a special "Shoe Box Service", where we pray for all the people involved – both in this country and overseas. This emotional service ensures that more than a thousand boxes from our church alone receive an enthusiastic send-off. We often watch a DVD of previous years' distributions and it is heartwarming to see the expressions on the children's faces as they realise they are not forgotten by the outside world.

After all that hard work it is nice to know where the shoe boxes have gone, so this year we are harnessing modern technology to be able to "follow" each box, as people can print out an electronic barcode which will then trigger an e-mail to the sender when the box reaches its destination.

"Operation Christmas Child" only began in 1990 as the dream of one man, when he saw on the news the plight of a group of children abroad whose suffering seemed largely ignored by the world. He discovered an untapped resource of people wanting to help and show love through their gifts, as they try to build bridges of caring on an international scale. In the few years since the charity began, it has grown incredibly quickly. It has gathered a lot of support and enthusiasm up and down the country as well as farther afield, as shoe boxes are collected in America as well.

When I saw some toys in a local shop that I thought would be appropriate gifts for a shoe box, I told the shop assistant what I wanted them for.

"I wish I had thought of that before you," she said to me. "Now I will have to think of something else for my shoe box!"

I suggested some ideas for her, and this lady – someone I had never met before – went away with plenty of suggestions for suitable gifts.

It isn't just children overseas who are benefiting from these gifts. It is bringing people together in this country, too, exchanging ideas for craft or other gifts, knitting and sewing together, or chatting with other volunteer workers over a cup of tea as we spend time checking the boxes. We are united in prayer with so many others for the recipients all over the world and this non-stop activity is fuelled by the knowledge that we are working to make Christmas special for others. After all, the message of Christmas is all about giving, isn't it? ■

Thinkstockphotos.

A Country Calendar For Spring

■ Seville oranges are in season until February, having begun to ripen in December. Tonnes of them are shipped over to the UK, where they are considered to be the very best fruit for producing marmalade. This is owing to their high pectin content. Although Dundee manufacturer Keillers' famously claim to have invented marmalade, there are references to it in literature from before their time.

■ Did you grow up "pinch-punching" friends or family members on the first of every month? This old English tradition is not spread around the whole of the UK, but is thought to originate from a time when the ritual was considered to protect you from witches. Just don't forget to finish with "No returns" when you say it!

A dry March and a wet May fills barns and bays with corn and hay.

■ Easter is soon upon us, and carries a whole wealth of traditions with it. The word itself is of Anglo-Saxon origin, from "Eostre-monath" – or the "month of openings".

The reason we give eggs at Easter is because they represent new life, but the concept of the Easter bunny is another of Anglo-Saxon origin! The story goes that the Saxon goddess Eostre helped a wounded bird survive winter by turning it into a hare. That hare found it could still lay eggs, which it decorated each spring and left as offerings of thanks.

Brown hare.

The start of the season sees the return of the migrating birds from warmer climes. It's a long journey for many, but spare a thought for the Arctic Tern, which flies over 18,500 miles each year, travelling between its breeding ground in the Arctic and alternate home in Antarctica!

FACT

March used to be the first month of the year. Before the adoption of the Gregorian calendar in 1600 in Scotland and 1752 in England and the switch to January 1, the start of March and its heralding of spring and regrowth meant it was a natural place to begin a new year.

Head to Lanark, Scotland on March 1 and you may be lucky enough to see the celebrations on Whuppity Scoorie Day! At 6 p.m., a bell is rung and a gathering of local children starts charging around the church in an anti-clockwise direction, making noise and swinging paper balls on strings above their heads.

As with all the most interesting traditions, nobody is totally sure where the practice originates, but the most likely explanation seems to be that it was a way of welcoming in spring and frightening off any remaining evil winter spirits!

The Daffodils

WE are the dancing daffodils,
The very breath of spring!
We come to keep you company,
Both joy and hope we bring.
We are the season's compliments,
Our gift is golden cheer,
Because we herald sunny days
To brighten up your year!

– ***Elizabeth Gozney.***

Thank You, Grandma

YOU opened doors to fairyland,
To distant places, far-off times,
To myths and magic, songs and games,
To long-lost stories, well-known rhymes.
You always listened to my tales,
We shared the laughter and the tears,
You seemed to know and understand
And eased the worries and the fears.

You told me I'm important, too,
When I was feeling rather low,
A special part of life's rich plan
With things to do and dreams to grow.
So thank you, Grandma, for your love,
It's always played a vital part.
Wherever in the world I go
You'll travel with me in my heart.

– Iris Hesselden.

The Welcome Sun

AT last we feel the welcome sun
As winter slips away,
And hope returns to lift our hearts
On this, the first warm day.
Green shoots are growing quickly now,
We see the earth awake,
The daffodils are dancing, too,
Beside the peaceful lake.

The birds are nesting in the trees
And butterflies appear,
The whole of life renewed once more.
Rejoice, for spring is here!
And, though the showers will return
And sometimes skies look grey,
Enjoy each moment in the sun
On this, the first warm day!

– ***Iris Hesselden.***

Blossom Of Springtime

WE stroll arm in arm
To enjoy the spring scene,
Between flowering trees
Mantled softly with green.
Bright, warming sun
Causes new sap to rise,
And each blossoming twig
Points its leaf to the skies.

Sweet almond blossom
Dispels winter gloom,
While the blackthorn enchants us
With fragile white bloom.
The cherry's pink petals
Drift softly to ground
And cling to our hair
As they float all around.

Bedecked with sweet blossom
Our walk we resume,
And I feel like a bride
On the arm of her groom!

– Maggie Smith.

Mum

ALWAYS loving,
Always caring,
Showed me kindness,
Taught me sharing.
Had a scare?
She'd be there.
Holding hands
In any weather,
Hurt a knee?
Kiss it better.

There to see if you're all right,
There with cuddles in the night.
Gave me sister, gave me brother,
Always giving, she's my mother.

– Antony Burr.

Into The Garden

NOW the springtime has returned
And winter months have passed,
It's time to turn my thoughts and mind
To gardening at last.
For spears of green and growing
shoots
Are thrusting through the ground,
The tired old earth has sprung to life
In secret – without sound.

The crocus cups, like coloured gems,
Have popped up everywhere,
And, peeping out midst gnarled roots,
A primrose here and there.
And all the trees in misted green
Are glistening with spring rain.
It's wonderful to be outside
In the garden once again.

– Kathleen Gillum.

Easter Joy

OUT over rooftops
Glad church bells are ringing;
In thick, greening hedges
Most small birds are singing;
While brown hares and rabbits,
With woolly lambs frolicking
Add to our joy in their play.

The primrose glows quietly,
Each celandine glossy;
In gardens and woodlands
Small green buds are sprouting;
With nature around us,
The new life proclaiming,
Let's celebrate Easter today!

– Maggie Smith.

from the Manse Window

The Changing Seasons

RECENTLY I went into a shop to buy a new bottle of my signature vanilla perfume that I wear every day, only to discover that they'd reformulated it by adding a touch of musk.

I dislike musk. It doesn't suit me at all. Now I have to look for a new perfume at a reasonable price. Why do they have to change things?

That's a common cry as we get older. We like things the way they are. Generally it's the young who embrace change and see it as exciting – upgrading their phones every week, or so it seems, while some of us have only just learned how to handle the internet and are quite happy to have computers that do the business without bells and whistles.

Yet everything changes; it's a fact of life. From the moment we're born we're on that rollercoaster of change, and no matter how much a mother might want to cling on to the baby stage in her child, it doesn't last.

The other day I drove my father to a hospital appointment. He looked at the city and reminisced about the way it was when he first arrived as a refugee over 50 years ago. He commented that if anybody who'd left all that time ago came back now they wouldn't recognise it. I remember feeling disappointed when my favourite department store closed down, and when the central gardens were replaced with a paved square, but things are always changing.

Many people dislike autumn because it's the end of summer and a long dark winter lies ahead. When I was younger it was my favourite season – the colours, the smoky smells, the crispness, the "mists and mellow fruitfulness". Yet, as I grow older, I prefer spring because of bluebells and blossom, light evenings and warmth, fresh green leaves on the trees and the promise of a long, lazy summer ahead. In autumn we can look forward to Advent and Christmas, the colours, the carols, candlelit churches, the smell of cinnamon and spice and roaring fires.

How boring life would be if it were endless summer! I've spent holidays on the west coast of America and in Florida with day after day of blue skies. When I return home I find myself welcoming our changeable climate, glad to experience rain.

It's easy to stagnate in our lives.

Thinkstockphotos.

By the Rev. Susan Sarapuk.

Often we have to be pushed into change for our own good. A few years ago I took a break from parish ministry after two curacies and five years as a vicar. I was out for about seven months until a former colleague invited me to work with him in his parish. I agreed.

On my first day back I sat alone eating my sandwiches, wondering what I'd done. Instead of a quiet life working from home, I'd been pitched back into a busy parish, and I didn't know whether I wanted to be. But as time went on I realised that I needed change, that I'd been stagnating without even realising it, and I came to enjoy the new challenge. I wouldn't have chosen it, but circumstances forced me to it and it was actually good for me. We've all experienced that in one way or another.

WE experience change in our Christian lives, as well, although you wouldn't think this in some churches which cling to the past as if the future is to be feared. There's the story of a vicar who wanted to move a piano from one spot in the church to another, but he knew there would be objections, so he moved it a few inches every week, and nobody noticed!

We like to cling to the comforting forms of service, the old hymns, the pews. In a rapidly changing world they provide the feeling of familiarity and constancy. These things are not bad in themselves, of course, but we also need to reach out to others and to see where God is leading us.

Change is often bewildering because we like things to run smoothly. We like things to go our way, when sometimes God has other plans for us. Think of Joseph, who was sold as a slave by his own brothers when he was a young boy. Consider all the struggles he went through. God used everything for a purpose, so that ultimately, when Joseph was reunited with his family after saving Egypt from famine, he could say of that terrible deed long ago, "You meant it for evil, but God meant it for good."

Now think of Jonah. When God told him to go one way, he decided he didn't like that idea and headed in the opposite direction – and look what he ran into! When he eventually did what God had asked him to, the things he'd feared didn't happen.

I'm sure Peter and the other disciples thought they were having a great time with Jesus and had their own plans for what would happen next. So when Jesus said he was going to Jerusalem where he'd be betrayed, arrested and killed, Peter said, "That'll never happen to you!"

This was not the way they saw things panning out. Possibly they imagined the kingdom was going to be in the here and now, in Jerusalem, where Jesus would be King and they, as his henchmen, would wield the sort of power they could only dream about. Things could only get better, so why was he talking about death?

Yet the death and resurrection of Jesus was God's rescue plan for the world. Even after the Resurrection Peter went back to fishing for a while – back to the familiar, the comfortable, because he couldn't cope with the changes he'd experienced.

Some changes can lead to a sense of diminishing and dying, just as when autumn gives way to winter. I think of Christians in the fledgling church in Jerusalem who were forced to leave their homes because of persecution. What a terrible time for them, a time when they might have questioned what God was doing. Yet it was through this that the good news spread throughout the Roman Empire, as they talked about Jesus wherever they ended up.

Sometimes in our walk of faith we go through what St John of the Cross referred to as the dark night of the soul, where nothing seems to work, God is far away, we feel useless and often we question our faith. That's a change we feel we can do without! But often God is taking us deeper, strengthening our faith when it seems weak, asking us if we're prepared to trust him.

Having to change my perfume is an inconvenience more than anything else, but it serves as a reminder that life is always changing. God is challenging us to change and grow, too. Just as autumn sows the seeds of spring, so in our times of dying and waiting in darkness, hope is sown and God's will is done, if we allow it. ■

Thinkstockphotos.

A Country Calendar For Spring

■ In the Cotswold town of Tetbury, the end of May and coming of summer is celebrated by a day of woolsack racing. In homage to the era when the town thrived as a market for wool, locals have been running as pairs and fours uphill between two pubs, carrying large sacks of the precious commodity. The men's bag weighs 27 kg and the women's 16 kg, and the event has become so popular that the fastest times are now recorded in the Guinness Book Of World Records!

■ Superstition used to draw young girls out on the first day of May to wash their faces in the morning dew. This was because of an old tale that anyone who washes with it will have a beautiful complexion all through the year!

April showers bring forth May flowers.

■ Tulips – one of the UK's most popular cut flowers – are beginning to appear in March. The word "tulip" comes from the Turkish for turban, because of their distinctive elegant shape.

FACT

The first day of spring in the southern hemisphere is the day of the autumnal equinox in the northern hemisphere! Isn't it nice to know that when things are winding down for winter in one part of the world, rebirth is just beginning in another?

■ The end of April sees the start of the short but sweet British asparagus season. Not only is it delicious, it also lives for a long time. The tender stems grow from "crowns" planted in the ground which have an active life of around 15 years! The oldest plant ever recorded reached the impressive age of 120 years . . .

■ Young rabbits are everywhere this time of year! They're a delightful sign of spring, and surely one of their most endearing traits is when they jump up and twist in an expression of joy. This is referred to as a "binky"!

Wild rabbit.

At Play

WHAT better sights on Easter Day
Than baby rabbits at their play?
Rabbits short and rabbits tall,
Rabbits large and rabbits small.
In and out of burrows round,
Up and down the hill they bound,
Their white tails bobbing in the sun,
As if to say, "Come join the fun."
If they could, I'm sure they'd sing,
So happy that, at last, it's spring;
Let's all give thanks for days so sunny,
And the joy of a new-born Easter bunny!

– Brian H. Gent.

Burgeoning Spring!

THE willows show a hint of green,
Such is the subtle change of scene,
Warmer blows the once-chill breeze
To breathe new life into the trees.
Little buds start to unfurl,
As from brown bracken fronds uncurl.
Full-throated thrush greet each new day,
And martins build their nests of clay,
So winter can no longer cling
Now a new spring is burgeoning.

– Brian H. Gent.

Little Lambs

STROLLING through the countryside
Beneath the sunny skies,
I look out on the pastoral scene
Spread before my eyes.
For all around are little lambs
In coats of fluffy white,
Jumping, frisking, gambolling –
To watch is pure delight.

With snowy coats contrasting
The verdant fields of green,
These energetic creatures
Enhance the springtime scene.
But now I must retrace my steps,
I turn to go my way,
And sadly I must bid farewell
To little lambs at play.

– Kathleen Gillum.

Peas, Please!

I **PLANTED** peas in March, I did,
An act of faith, with days so chill.
Yet still I sowed them with a will
And marked the muddy drill.

The days crept by, so damp and cold
I half forgot my enterprise
Until they took me by surprise –
I saw small seedlings rise.

Green leaves and tendrils reaching up.
I gave them canes to help them climb
And watched them closely, judging time
To pick them in their prime.

June sunshine, and the tender pods
Are ready now to pick and eat,
So green and round, so fresh and sweet,
Such bounty would be hard to beat –
The spring's most perfect treat!

– Maggie Ingall.

Summer

In Bloom

I **LOOK** out of my window
At the break of every dawn,
And see the misty halo of
A freshly dew-clad lawn.
I watch a perky robin
As he hops to and fro,
To find a tasty morsel
His red breast all aglow.
A badger lopes along the path;
Complete, his nightly quest,
To wend his way back to his sett
And take a well-earned rest.
A blackbird and a speckled thrush
Their daily duet trill,
Such is their sheer exuberance
That never fails to thrill.
There is a cheeky squirrel,
Bushy tail a-twitch,
Who comes to see me every morn
To daily life enrich.
Graceful goldfish languish
In a tranquil, lilied pond,
And blue wisteria tassles
Entwine the wall beyond.
Bumblebees and butterflies
Busy 'mongst the flowers,
Bring wondrous ways of nature
To while away the hours.
What more could one wish for
To dispel winter's gloom,
Than a country garden
When it is in full bloom?

– ***Brian H. Gent.***

Wild Poppies

THOUGH the poets sing your praises,
Farmers look on you with scorn
When you thread your scarlet ribbons
Through their fields of ripening corn.
Little poppies, silken poppies,
Pert and pretty as you please,
Like tiny Romanies you greet us,
Red skirts fluttering in the breeze.

Black-eyed peonies, ever cheerful,
Bright as paint and full of fun,
How it lifts the heart to see you
Dancing gaily in the sun!
Though you cannot vie in beauty
With your sisters, it is true,
No other flower can hold a candle
To the brilliance of your hue.

Evocative of deeds of glory,
In a darker, bygone year,
Though bittersweet the thoughts you kindle,
One and all we hold you dear.
Many a tired old face will soften,
Remembering some well-loved name,
At the sight of one wild poppy
Glowing, steadfast as a flame.

– ***Kathleen O'Farrell.***

The Sundial

IT was old when I was young,
The wind and rain had etched its face
And tarnished the metal
But the time still passes.

Children skipped and danced around its base,
Laughing and happy,
And I was there those long years ago,
But drifting away like a shadow I was gone,
But not its shadow.

There was no key or whirling wheels,
No steady tick, tick of time,
Just the exclusion of sun across its face,
A shadow, in quiet commitment.

It came from a bygone age,
When things were simpler,
Easier to understand,
But my sundial is timeless
And like its shadow is complete.

– J. Pirie.

Sunflower Summer

GREAT heads of gold,
And standing bold
While reaching for the sky.
Such tall green towers,
With glorious flowers,
Quite dazzling to the eye!
Slowly turning,
Ever yearning,
Eager for the sun.
By warm rays blest,
You take no rest,
Till summer days are done.

– Maggie Smith.

from the Manse Window

Waiting For God

THERE'S a TV advert for a well-known brand of confectionery where children are faced with a sweet and told that if they can resist eating it for a certain length of time then they can have another one. It's based on a real child psychology test to determine how certain personality traits emerge in children; whether it's nature or nurture.

Needless to say, in the experiment many children can't wait and eat the sweet almost immediately. Yet, those who can resist seem to show greater degrees of self-control and self-discipline in other areas, too.

Waiting is hard, particularly for children, and especially so at Christmas. I was one of those children who enjoyed the waiting and anticipation and wanted to be surprised, but I had friends in school who would hunt high and low to discover all their presents before Christmas Day arrived.

I wonder what it must have been like for Mary waiting for Jesus to be born. What was this thing growing inside her? Was she delusional? Perhaps she'd imagined Gabriel's visit. Maybe it had been no more than a dream, or maybe she was going mad! And if what the angel had said did come to pass, what sort of future were she and Joseph going to have? Would anybody believe her when she said her boy was the Son of God?

Joy and apprehension must have been intermingled. It was definitely uncharted territory. But we get the impression that Mary was a very level-headed young girl – after all, she didn't seem to be frightened by Gabriel's message and she complied with faith – "Let it be to me as you have said."

Nor did the waiting end after the birth of Jesus. It took 30 years for him to begin his ministry. Can you imagine what those 30 years of waiting were like for Mary, wondering about the words of Simeon's prophecy – "And a sword will pierce your own heart"?

Sometimes she must have hoped that her son would have an ordinary life, after all. Perhaps it was easy to believe that would be so, as she brought up her young family living a simple life. We know that Jesus took up the trade of his father and became a carpenter. As the years went by, Mary might have hoped that he would settle down with his own

Thinkstockphotos.

By the Rev. Susan Sarapuk.

family, and that all the promises, prophecies and wondrous things that had happened so long ago would remain in the past.

Mary had to learn the lesson of waiting, for everything is in God's time and he does not forget his promises.

"Wait for the Lord," the psalmist exhorts. "Be strong and take heart and wait for the Lord."

Even as the oppressed Jewish nation under the Romans was crying out for deliverance and asking, "How long, Lord?" Jesus was being born. Although the deliverance he would eventually bring was not the physical and political solution they were seeking, it would be something much greater, more than anyone could have imagined. But God's people had not been forgotten.

With God there is always the right time.

When the time had fully come, God sent his son, the Apostle Paul writes.

Why was this the right time? The Roman Empire was in control of most of the known world; they'd built roads, there was a common administrative language, the lines of communication were open and people of different nations had been brought together under one umbrella. People were ready to hear and change.

THE Bible has quite a lot to say about God's timing. In our modern society we want things now. We order something off the internet and it'll be delivered the following day. We queue for more than five minutes and we begin to get restless. Sometimes my computer is slow and it drives me nuts! We get into debt because, rather than save up for something, we can have it now if we use our credit card. This seems to be particularly prevalent at Christmas, when people are under pressure to give their families a happy festive period.

We have to learn to live by God's timing, to wait for what he's going to do and not give up hope. Sometimes that seems hard, in a time when church attendance is declining and we don't know what to do about it, when the Christian consensus in our land seems to be disintegrating.

It's not a new problem. Quite a few of the Old Testament prophets cried out in despair because they could see no way forward, and God had to encourage them that all was not lost, that there were still people who believed and that things would happen in His time. Sometimes we forget that we don't see the whole picture.

"God is working his purpose out as year succeeds to year", the old hymn reminds us.

As the prophet Habbakuk reminded people about the vision of the future, "Though it linger, wait for it: it will certainly come and not delay."

We have to wait because we're not ready, and that's just a part of life. When we're growing up there are many things we want to do, but we're not mature enough to handle them. I remember I was in a hurry to take my driving test, but my instructor knew that I wasn't quite ready, even though I felt I was. I failed the first time and passed the second.

Waiting can be an expression of faith. We choose to believe that God is faithful and that He will fulfil his promises, no matter what the world around us is saying. Often our faith is judged harshly by society. People say there's no evidence that there's a God, or they ask the question, "How can there be a God when there is so much suffering?"

That might have been the sentiment of the crowd gathered around the Cross, jeering as Jesus hung there with his mother weeping at what it had come to. And yet that was the very moment, when all seemed lost, that everything was being won.

People couldn't see it then. Afterwards, it became clear to those who wanted to see. Afterwards, Mary understood everything. Yes, a sword had pierced her heart, but what joy was to follow! All in God's time.

Waiting is not meant to be done in a vacuum. After the birth of Jesus and the incredible visits of the wise men and shepherds, we're told that "Mary pondered all these things in her heart". She reflected and she prayed.

So we don't moan that God has forgotten us, that He has forgotten this broken world where evil so often appears to triumph. We are positive in our faith, waiting and praying, ready to hear God's voice and see what He will do at the right time.

Children wait for Christmas with anticipation – let's be honest, adults do, too! – and when it arrives there is much joy. Mary waited, and when Jesus arrived there was much joy. We wait for good things and for what God has personally promised to us. It will come, but it is always in God's time.

"Blessed are those who wait for Him!" ■

Thinkstockphotos.

A Country Calendar For *Summer*

June marks the start of summer proper, the season of plenty, and nothing says summer more than the beginning of the British strawberry season.

Did you know, though, that at the Wimbledon Tennis Championship alone roughly 27,000 kilograms of them are eaten?

■ The start of summer sees the beginning of festival season, and one that is growing ever more popular is Hay-on-Wye's spectacular Festival of Literature and the Arts. Described by Bill Clinton as a "Woodstock for the mind", it draws the biggest names in literature, and now organises similar events around the world in places as far-flung as Bogota and Nairobi!

A calm June puts the farmer in tune.

Ready for action.

■ There's a good chance that, at the many summer events taking place around the country, you might come across Morris dancers. Very little is known about the origins of this folk dance, but today it is a popular fixture at village fêtes. Records indicate that a man called William Kemp once performed a solo dance all the way from London to Norwich in 1600.

Summer is a great time to view sea life in Britain's coastal waters. The Scottish coast is a good place to start, with whales making their presence known in the Minches of the west coast, and regular sightings of dolphins in the food-rich waters off Chanonry Point near Inverness.

FACT

Mid-August this year will see an impressive meteor shower in the constellation of Perseus, with anything up to 60 per hour at its peak. In some central European countries they believed it signified someone's passing when one fell, meaning it was common to hear folk uttering blessings when they were seen.

Every year at the Summer Solstice, crowds are drawn to Stonehenge to watch the sun come up. Stonehenge is reckoned to be between 4,000 and 5,000 years old, but archaeologists discovered evidence that the site has held special significance for up to 10,000 years!

Stonehenge.

Sweet Perfume

IT isn't in a bottle,
It isn't in a jar,
And to find its equal
You'd have to travel far.
It always takes you by surprise,
Part of its special charm,
The perfume, so compelling,
Is like a soothing balm.
Money cannot buy it,
No glossy "ad" displays
That sweetness wafted on the breeze
By a field of new-mown hay.

– ***Brian H. Gent.***

A Cold Drink And A Good Book

THERE'S really nothing like it
On a sunny summer's day,
To get outside with a good book
And pass the hours away.
To feel the cool breeze on your neck,
And sense the sun's warm kiss,
Relaxing with an ice-cold drink –
This surely must be bliss.
There's nothing so delightful
As a quiet and shady nook,
While sitting in the garden
With a cold drink and a book.

– Kathleen Gillum.

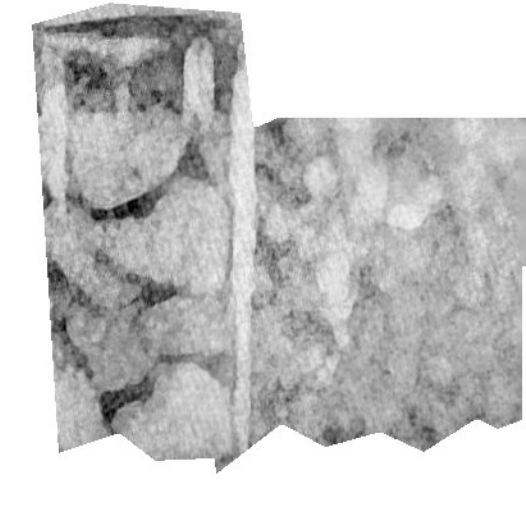

Standing Side By Side

THE beach huts all in pretty colours,
Standing side by side,
Observe like silent sentinels
The ever-changing tide.
And deckchairs with their stripey seats
Are parked along the sand,
So people can sit and relax
And hear the big brass band.

Seashells, sand and sailing ships,
The rockpools, cliffs and caves,
The bobbing boats, the balmy breeze
And sound of lapping waves.
The crying gulls that dip and dive,
The salty tang of spray,
Are all part of the seaside scene
When on my holiday.

– Kathleen Gillum.

Holiday Time!

I'M off tomorrow. Cheerio!
But what to pack? I just don't know.
A sun hat? Yes, I think I will;
And what about a sea-sick pill?
Well, no, that's daft. I'll go by road.
But is my swimsuit safely stowed?
And are my flip-flops packed as well?
My sponge bag and my shower gel?
Oh, underwear! I quite forgot!
I think I'll just throw in the lot.
One book or two? Let's make it three –
I like to read beside the sea.
Some choccy bars and sucky sweets
(Well, what's a hol without some treats?)
Some handkerchiefs to blow my nose,
Biscuits, and what else? Ah, clothes!
This panic strikes each time I roam.
I think, next year, I'll just stay home!

– Maggie Ingall.

A Taste Of Summer

THE family, strolling to and
  fro
Along the promenade,
Are sipping drinks of apple
  juice
And fragrant lemonade;
Licking orange lollipops,
And chocolate ice-cream,
With sticks of rock and
  candyfloss
An awesome pink daydream!

There are beefburgers and hot
  dogs
With other goodies, too,
While Gran sits calmly in her
  chair,
The seashore in her view.
She is watching all the
  movements
Of her younger family,
Her Thermos at the ready
With a welcome cup of tea!

– ***Maggie Smith.***

ICE
CREAM

Ladies' Day

THEY stroll on the lawns
With an elegant air,
Displaying slim figures
Of fashion with flair.

While babies their afternoon
Slumbers are taking,
Small girls sit happily
Daisy-chain-making.

Their brothers are stealthily
Creeping through trees,
While Grandad's loud snores
Waft away on the breeze.

Time in the garden,
All kitchens forsaken,
For the men tend the barbecues –
Burgers and bacon!

– ***Maggie Smith.***

A Summer Downpour

SILENT, silent as a ghost it came
Upon the unsuspecting crowd.
Dark, dark as the Underworld
Came the weighed-down, moisture-laden cloud.
Those people who, with bucket and spade
Admired the sandcastles they had made.
Or, while playing in the sea,
Splashed with innocence and glee,
Unaware of the menace to their fun.
The cloud filled the sky, ate up the sun,
Released some raindrops, made them run.
Like panicked ants they grabbed their things –
Towels and clothes and floating rings,
Seeking shelter along the shore.
Run for cover! It will pour!
And sploosh! Watch the wall of water go!
Drench the old, the lame, the slow,
And then, bare minutes since it started,
The rain had stopped, the clouds had parted,
And those who had been slow to run,
Were left there, dripping in the sun.

– ***Antony Burr.***

from the Manse Window

Nature At Work

IT was nobody's fault, just nature at work, doing what it does naturally. Years before we moved in, a sycamore seed must have landed on top of the manse wall, taken root, and now a huge, spreading tree dominated the skyline.

While the autumn colours were admittedly beautiful, we had barrow-loads of leaves to clear up every year. Not only did it block out the summer evening sunlight, its roots had grown down through the stones and begun to burst the wall. Large chunks of masonry were beginning to fall into the neighbouring property several feet below.

The Congregational Committee had it on the agenda, and were looking understandably anxious until a nice lady from next door came round and asked would we mind if they took it on themselves to build a new wall.

Did we mind? Not at all!

"Tear away! Yes, of course you can have access from our side, no problem!" we said with enthusiasm.

So it has been an interesting few weeks, very educational for ourselves and our Alsatian dog, who has had to get used to observing the builders a few feet from her nose through a temporary fence.

We have together watched first the tree and then the old stonework being taken down and away and a magnificent new structure built in its place. We now have a lot more light and a bright, solid pebble-dashed wall topped with a shiny metal fence that will probably be standing a lot longer than any of us!

One casualty has been the garden. Admittedly, the shrubbery had got a bit wild and overgrown, but with the demolition and all the trampling about, it became a scene of real devastation! We've actually lost quite a bit of what we'd planted over the years.

The hydrangea is in bits, literally, and the butterflies are missing their buddleia bush. What was, up to recently, abundant foliage and blossom is now just empty space. About a dozen bushes remain and frankly they look fairly traumatised.

But am I worried? Not overly. Because I believe in resurrection.

"Christ has indeed been raised from the dead, the first fruits of those who have fallen asleep," the New Testament affirms confidently (1 Corinthians 15 v 20).

Thinkstockphotos.

By the Rev. Andrew Watson.

Death is not the end of the story. Jesus's disciples witnessed their master crucified, killed and buried, yet on the third day they met him alive again, strong, victorious.

Christ died and rose again from death and ascended to glory. Those who trust in him are instructed in the Bible to expect nothing less!

And if you think about it, it's almost as if God has built an annual reminder of resurrection into the natural order He created.

OBSERVE the seasons. Every autumn the trees shed their leaves, winter leaving them stark and bare. They look dead, finished. How could they ever come again? Yet every year spring faithfully comes around, the frost retreats and the branches bud once more! That which seemed dead and gone for ever returns to bloom again.

Look out of your window as the days begin to lengthen and perhaps you can see snowdrops and daffodils, springing from earth that, just a few weeks ago, was frozen solid. An annual reminder from the Creator of the miracle of resurrection.

So there's hope for our garden. I'll trim the remaining bushes back, maybe plant a few new ones, dig over the soil a bit, and wait for nature to prove as reliable as ever.

And we're off to a good start – our wonderful neighbours even got the builders to spread some new topsoil for us and gave us something towards purchasing new shrubs!

Therefore I will not lie awake worrying about it, nor prod the ground impatiently every day with a hoe. I'll just keep faith in nature. And by this time next year I've no doubt things will be flourishing and looking better than ever.

We should equally try not to lose heart when God, in His wisdom, brings us through periods of "winter" in our lives. No-one wishes for harsh and painful times, but they seem inevitable to some degree in this present world.

We are assured these won't be the end of the story. We are living in anticipation of an eternal "spring", resurrected to be with the Lord, which the New Testament tells us is much better.

Part of John's vision in Revelation 22 of the new Heavens and Earth is of the "Tree of Life". Not a wild, destructive sycamore, like the problem one we had, but an eternal source of life and wholeness. "The tree of life, bearing twelve crops of fruit, yielding its fruit every month. And the leaves of the tree are for the healing of the nations."

No more aches, pains or sorrow ever again.

Meantime, these trials can be taken as opportunities to simplify; to prune back some of the less helpful things in our lives and trust more closely the Lord Jesus, who also suffered so much on our behalf!

In John 15 Jesus uses another horticultural image, saying: "I am the true vine, and my Father is the gardener. He cuts off every branch in me that bears no fruit, while every branch that does bear fruit He prunes so that it will be even more fruitful."

Sometimes, ironic as it may seem, it's when life has dealt us a humbling blow, when we've had to sacrifice something dear to us, when we're feeling weak or vulnerable, that we are most inclined to really trust and follow closely our Lord. And in so doing we actually can become far more useful and fruitful in God's service.

God used the apparent weakness and defeat of the Cross to save the world! He can use us, even in our periods of suffering, to bless and encourage others. How often this has been the case, when I've gone to visit someone in a time of need, and come away feeling they have encouraged me much more than I them!

The Apostle Paul shares, in Corinthians, a distressing situation he faced. We're not told exactly what it was but he describes it as a "thorn in the flesh".

He pleaded with God to take it away, but gradually learned to trust and even rejoice through it, discovering that God's grace is sufficient for us, that His power is found most effective in our times of weakness.

My poor garden may look a bit sad and weak just at the moment, but I believe all sorts of wonderful things are already happening microscopically just under the surface, and I'm looking forward to seeing all that is going to burst forth by Easter.

Whatever challenges you're facing in your life just now, let springtime and Easter encourage you to fresh hope. Our Lord is risen indeed, and we are promised to share in that glory. Meanwhile, he is with us, graciously at work in us, even in times of apparent frailty, to fulfil his good purposes for us and those about us. As nature blossoms around us, unstoppable, let hope, thanks and praise to the Lord be our constant theme! ■

Thinkstockphotos.

A Country Calendar For Summer

■ The recent wet summers have been hard on the butterfly population, but they remain a steadfast symbol of summer throughout the world. In fact, Antarctica is the only continent on the planet that doesn't have any representatives from the butterfly or moth family. Hardly surprising given that butterflies in particular can't fly if their body temperature is below 30 deg. C., 86 deg. F.!

■ Summer fêtes always have a range of games, often including the traditional coconut shy. This pastime has a long history in this country, and dates from the time when coconuts were highly prized and exotic commodities. The word "shy" is an old-fashioned term for throwing!

■ This summer sees the start of the Glasgow Commonwealth Games, running for two weeks from July 23. The Games have their origin in the British Empire Games, which were originally held to bring together the nations of the Empire, and to this day athletes carry a baton from Buckingham Palace to the opening ceremony of the games, wherever it may be.

Thinkstockphotos.

As we Brits know, summer doesn't necessarily guarantee blue skies! Ironically, though, the umbrella was invented to provide shade from the sun, and Europeans adapted them, making them from wood or whalebone and covering them in alpaca or canvas to provide protection from damp conditions!

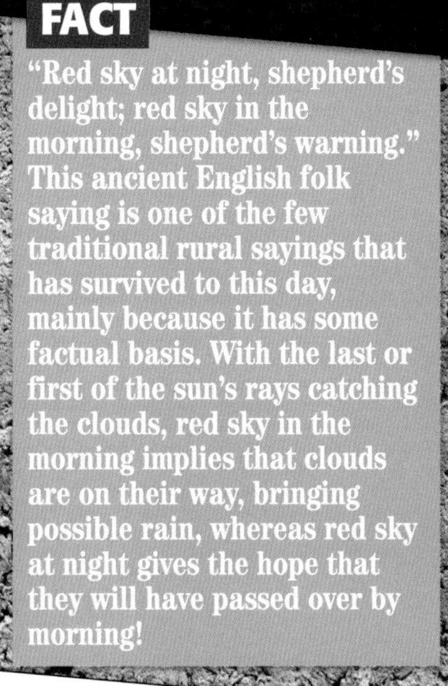

FACT

"Red sky at night, shepherd's delight; red sky in the morning, shepherd's warning." This ancient English folk saying is one of the few traditional rural sayings that has survived to this day, mainly because it has some factual basis. With the last or first of the sun's rays catching the clouds, red sky in the morning implies that clouds are on their way, bringing possible rain, whereas red sky at night gives the hope that they will have passed over by morning!

British peas hit their stride at this time of year. Podding fresh peas can be very relaxing, and would have been a regular chore in days gone by. Did you know that finding nine peas in a pod was considered good luck?

Fresh as can be.

A Flight Of Fancy

I SAT one summer eve
At Richmond, beer in hand,
And watched the queues of planes
Drop slowly out the sky, to land
At Heathrow, close to where I sat,
And wondered from what distant shore
These craft had come and, furthermore,
Where could they bear a traveller to?
Once a perilous trip of weeks;
Now a day, no more, would do.
My mind took flight. I could, perchance,
Be in a tavern in southern France,
And in my hand, not beer but wine,
Crushed nearby from local vine.
Or maybe I could drink my fill
With alpine view in Wilderswil.
But why stop there? Farther afield
The thought of New York bars appealed,
Or, midst sweltering heat and desert sand,
An Aussie lager would be grand.
Still the planes came one by one,
Golden in the setting sun.
Bringing folk from far-off lands,
Who'd dreamed of sitting, beer in hand
In a Thames-side tavern, like the one
Where I sat, dreaming in the sun.

– Antony Burr.

FRESH

Picnic In The Park

THE children are excited,
Looking forward to this day.
They really hope the sun will shine,
The rain will stay away.
They packed their bags and cases,
But Mum's been busy, too –
So many snacks and crisps and drinks
They all need quite a few.

So now they're ready, off they go
As happy as the lark,
To feed the ducks and go on swings
And picnic in the park.
There's happiness and friendliness
With families together,
They share the beauty and the fun
In sunny summer weather.

But soon it's time to head for home
Before it's really dark,
The children sleep and dream again
Of picnics in the park!

– Iris Hesselden.

Castles By The Sea

THE seagull's cry,
A clear blue sky,
When you and me
Played by the sea.
Those castles grand
Of silver sand,
And moats we made
With wooden spade,
Toy yachts moored,
Rock pools explored,
To catch a glimpse
Of crabs and shrimps,
Rocks, seaweed-hung,
When we were young
And days were long
And full of song;
Still memory stays
Of holidays
That you and me
Spent by the sea.

– Brian H. Gent.

The Fête

SKIPPING, laughing and chattering,
Clinging on to their mother's hand,
The boys and girls excitedly
Outside the school gate, stop and stand.
At last it was their special day,
For they had planned this summer fête,
Today no lessons, lots of play.
Hurry! Begin! They couldn't wait.

For on this day, the teachers said
Each class could run their different stalls,
And having made and painted them
They'd placed them round their classroom walls.
A hoopla stall with great big rings;
Boxes to stand the prizes on;
They'd made some flags and hung them up,
Placed all the skittles one by one.

Their cardboard money was such fun,
Real coconuts they'd try make fall,
And in some baskets they could throw
A soft but very bouncy ball.
Then in the playground they must pay
To go on swings and climbing frame,
And the great scarecrow man they'd made
Won prizes if you guessed his name.

The gates were opened; in they rushed,
So shiny-eyed, each girl and boy.
They paid to pin on donkey's tail,
Refreshments, cakes! What fun! What joy!
The money they knew wasn't real,
They spent it, had change, it was great!
How proud they were, what fun they had;
Today they'd run their own school fête!

– Chrissy Greenslade.

Harvest Hymn

THANK you for the bounty, Lord,
That you bestow each year,
To feed us through the winter months
That are so cold and drear.
The grain is stored safe in the barn
And waiting for the mill;
Reward for honest, calloused hands
That hoe and plough and till.
Ripened fruit is on display
In church and chapel stalls,
Whilst golden sheaves of wheat and barley
Decorate the walls,
Saffron-coloured pumpkins, and
Bright green marrows, too,
With peas and beans and aubergines
Arranged for us to view.
So at this Harvest Festival,
We thank you, Lord, once more,
For all the gifts that you bestow
To make our spirits soar.

– Brian H. Gent.

The Gift Of Laughter

WE all need laughter now and then,
We need a smile or two
To see the brighter side of life
And let the sun shine through.
We need to share a friendly word
With people every day,
To spread a little cheerfulness
As we go on our way.

We need to look for hopefulness,
A rainbow after rain,
To keep an optimistic view,
Then dreams are not in vain.
We all need laughter in our lives;
It warms us deep within.
So share a little happiness
And let the smiles begin!

– Iris Hesselden.

Last Day Of The Holidays

I'VE been to the beach and I've been to the park,
I've been to the fair and come home after dark,
But now school's beginning; the holidays end.
It's like a bereavement, like losing a friend.

I've got a new teacher; forgotten her name.
It doesn't really matter, they're all much the same.
But it won't be so bad once we've made a start;
After all, there is football and playtime and art.

Although we do fractions, times tables and sums,
On Wednesday there's snacks and iced sticky buns,
And I found it quite interesting that time that we read
About what Egyptians once did with their dead.

I've missed seeing Adam, who has sweets every day.
He always comes up with some great game to play.
I've missed Dan, who likes dragons, and Tom with his trains,
And Harry who always stays in when it rains.

So, although term's beginning and the holiday ends,
It won't be too bad to get back with my friends.

– Antony Burr.

A Hint Of Morning Mist

IT'S lovely to go walking out
On cooler autumn days,
When there's a hint of morning mist
Which turns to golden haze.
A time when trees are shedding leaves
Their colours bold and bright,
And spiders' webs hold gems of dew
All sparkling in the light.

A nimble squirrel buries nuts,
He hardly makes a sound
As conkers with their chestnut sheen
Come plopping to the ground.
When fruited boughs are laden down
And trees are all ablaze,
I do enjoy just taking walks
On crisp and cooler days.

– Kathleen Gillum.

from the Manse Window

Beauty In The Bombsite

DURING the war, London was bombed night after night by German planes. Many buildings were destroyed, whole streets suffered and familiar landmarks disappeared. Rubbish lay everywhere together with burned-out rubble and massive craters where bombs had exploded.

Much of the city lay in ruins and it seemed as if the land had become dead and waste. The war years cast a grey blanket over our childhood, for we lived in Kent beneath the flight path of hostile aircraft heading for London.

It meant troubled nights crouching in a cupboard under the stairs whilst Spitfires and Mosquitos fought battles in the sky above our heads. The days were disturbed by the harsh wail of the air-raid warning siren and the loud blast of the all-clear.

School lessons were often held in the shelter and on occasion we would have to run from the classroom and dive into safety, though none of us children liked the damp, cold, concrete refuge. Often we were plucked from our beds in the middle of the night by anxious parents and carried to safety.

One unpopular occurrence was gas-mask drill conducted by a member of the Home Guard. We were frightened by the masks and only half understood the fearful truth behind the reason we had to carry them around.

When a Doodlebug crashed in the vicinity we would hop on our bikes, tear off to the site and pick up a souvenir of metal. If you found one with German writing on it, you would show it proudly to your friends in the playground.

By the end of the war I had a cardboard box full of bits and pieces. Food was strictly rationed and on my first day at boarding school we breakfasted on bread and grey-coloured dripping, followed by a lunch of split pea soup and an evening meal of corned beef with tinned tomatoes. All in all it was a worrying and fear-filled time.

SOON after the war something amazing happened. In fact, it would not be an exaggeration to say that a miracle was played out in front of our eyes. All over the bomb craters, a haze of green appeared.

Thinkstockphotos.

By the Rev. David Bryant.

Flowers started to grow out of the rubble and waste and birds and butterflies began to brighten the wasteland. Clumps of bright yellow ragwort sprang up. Bracken sprouted from the earth and grasses once again waved in the breeze.

Many of the older generation of Londoners will remember the great swathes of bright pink rosebay willowherb flowering luxuriantly where the bombs had done their destructive work. The dreadful desolation wrought by the war was slowly being transformed and a garden of Eden was blossoming forth, undoing the horror of night-time raids.

Even more remarkable was a small bird that came into these once unlovely places to make a home. It was an uncommon visitor from Denmark and the Baltic. The black redstart built a nest, laid eggs and reared its young in the craters and it became affectionately known as the bombsite bird. Hitler's bombing raids had proved unable to stop the great surge of God's creation from renewing the wilderness. It was as if spring could not be held back by any human wickedness.

It reminded me of a hope-filled passage from the book of Isaiah in which the prophet describes the coming of the Lord.

"The wilderness and the dry land shall be glad, the desert shall rejoice and blossom; like the crocus it will blossom abundantly and rejoice with joy and singing. They shall see the glory of the Lord, the majesty of God."

Other memories float back from the past of glorious springtimes when the world seemed to burst out afresh in joy at the end of winter. When the war ended and it was safe to roam outside once again, we Sunday school children were taken to a nearby wood to gather moss and pick primroses with which to decorate the Easter garden in church.

Later we placed the pottery figures of Jesus, Mary and the disciples next to the empty tomb amongst the flowers and moss. It was usually turned into a half-day outing complete with a picnic brought by the adults. Rugs were spread out in the wood, sandwiches, cakes and Thermoses were produced and lemonade powder was stirred into bottles of water.

We sat down in the wood with the glories of spring around us. There were leaves bursting out on the trees, woodland butterflies fluttering in glades, wild flowers and singing birds. Once, I remember my father pointing out a rare hairstreak butterfly. Sometimes we climbed trees and looked down on spring from the great height of a horse chestnut or oak. Even as a child I could sense the wonders of nature.

THEN I remember a holiday spent with our two young children in Spain. There had been a dreadful storm with flooding, thunder, lightning, high winds and no electricity. One day the cloud lifted, the Mediterranean sun appeared again and we took a little train along the coast to Alicante. The carriages trundled gently past a sea of orange and lemon trees in full blossom, mile after mile of it, and I have never forgotten this marvellous sight.

London, you might think, is not the best place in which to enjoy a burgeoning spring. But even in the heart of that metropolis there is an awakening after winter. For nine years I used to drive to work early every morning past Marble Arch, that busy junction of roads right in the heart of the capital.

There was a scrubby patch of grass in the centre of the roundabout surrounded day and night by ceaseless traffic and crowds. During the winter months it lay dormant and sodden. Then, almost overnight – usually during March – a change took place. The whole area burst out into a riot of crocuses, yellow, white and purple, transforming it. How it lifted my spirits on a dank, drab Monday morning.

Spring brings joy the world over. Some three thousand years ago an unknown writer in the Song of Songs described the love of God as being like the first signs of spring.

"For lo, the winter is past, the rain is over and gone, the flowers appear on earth, the time of singing has come and the voice of the turtledove is heard in our land. The fig tree puts forth its figs and the vines are in blossom, they give forth fragrance."

Spring is indeed a beautiful time of budding flowers, blossoming trees, nest-building birds and vegetables stirring in the allotment. Above all, it is a time to spend a few prayerful moments thanking God for the glory of the world and the wonder of his creation. ■

Thinkstockphotos.

A Country Calendar For *Autumn*

■ Harvest festivals exist all over the world, giving thanks for the rich fruits of the land. In the United States it is a public holiday as well, and is called "Thanksgiving". Although turkey is the customary centrepiece to a Thanksgiving meal, it's traditional for the President to officially "pardon" one turkey, which will then be allowed to spend the remainder of its days roaming free.

■ Come autumn, Northamptonshire plays host to the World Conker Championships. Organised by Ashton Conker Club, the competition has been going for nearly 50 years now. Forget all your home remedies for preparing rock-hard conkers, though – all the conkers and laces are provided by the club!

Dull November brings the blast, Then the leaves are whirling fast

Job done.

■ The ceremony, "Calling The Mare", was a lovely custom that had farmers who had finished gathering their crops make a rough mare shape out of their last sheaf. They would then drop it into fields where other farmers were still working, shout "Mare! Mare!" and run away. The idea was that the wild horses would eat their crops if they didn't hurry up and finish the job.

With the trees in their colourful seasonal coats, it's no wonder many a poet has been inspired by this time of year.

"Season of mists and mellow fruitfulness, Close bosom-friend of the maturing sun," opens Keats' famous poem "To Autumn". This was inspired by a walk from beautiful Winchester, which is now marked for everyone to be inspired by!

FACT

As the squirrels start to bury their food for the months ahead, you might spot them licking it or rubbing it against their face before they do. It is this scent-marking that allows them to find it again!

A sign of things to come.

Michaelmas Day lands on September 29, and it's said that "If St Michael brings many acorns, Christmas will cover the fields with snow."

Baking Day

EGGS and butter and sugar and spice,
Flour and flavouring, too.
For making superior pastries and cakes
Only the best will do!

Creaming the butter with sugar and eggs,
Mixing the flour with the spice.
It's lovely to think that the cakes that we make
Will taste so exceedingly nice.

Making the pastry for tartlets or pies,
Preparing their fillings with care,
Enjoying the thought of the pleasure they'll give
When the fruits of our labours we share.

There's great satisfaction in spending some hours
Producing these nice tasty things,
And when folk enjoy them, it's lovely to see
The pleasure that Baking Day brings!

– Rosemary Bennett.

Cottage Delights

THE cottage, with its roof of thatch,
Is warm and welcoming.
Light streams from lattice window-panes,
Enticing, beckoning.
In cosy rooms with chintzy chairs
The table's set for tea.
A log fire blazes in the hearth
And crackles cheerily.

Bright cushions, rugs and rows of books
And pictures here and there
Have all been placed by loving hands
With thoughtfulness and care.
In this atmosphere of peace
And calm tranquillity,
A sense of warmth and sweet content
Steals quietly over me.

– *Kathleen Gillum.*

Woodland Walks

WOODLAND walks in windy weather,
Leaves awhirl as branches blow,
Autumn colours, rich as gemstones –
Nature gives her finest show.
Skies grow gold as sun sinks lower,
Shadows stretching long and low,
Time to pause and turn our footsteps.
Far we've come, and far to go.
Home at last, and firelight dancing.
Mugs of chocolate? We won't say no!
Sweet and warm with melting mallows;
Day departs in perfect glow.

– *Maggie Ingall.*

Swallow Dale

AMAZING hues tint autumn days
When bronzing bracken seems to blaze,
The valleys veiled in mellow haze
On Swallow Dale.

Now we see the swallows throng
On roofs and barns with cheery song.
They weaved the air all summer long
With grace and skill.

Sadly we watch them fly away,
Following the flock to some bright new day.
The months pass by, the skies turn grey
With snow and hail.

Awaiting the spring sun, warm and strong,
The swallows return to where they belong,
Filling the air with joyful song
Above Swallow Dale.

– ***Maggie Smith.***

Magic Stillness

I **STOOD** and watched the leaves of brown
And gold and crimson spiral down.
With fading flowers here and there
A tranquil magic filled the air,
As if to say the time is near
To mark the ending of the year.
The fruit has ripened on the bough,
And all is still and quiet now.
Vegetation past its best
Now needs to take a well-earned rest.
So it will be, until the day
We see white snowdrops on display.

– Brian H. Gent.

The Necklace

THE fun is in the finding, half hidden in the drifts,
Yet sharp eyes soon espy them, the chestnut tree's bright gifts.
Each treasure, round and shining, is plunged inside their bag,
As Molly and her grandad collect their autumn swag.

The skill is in the making, so now the thing to do
Is take their treasure homeward, to drill them neatly through.
So deft are Grandad's fingers; so clever and so fleet
As Molly watches closely, his task is soon complete.

The joy is in the threading. Each one's an outsized pearl!
They're working hard together, are Grandad and the girl;
In mutual concentration the time flies quickly past.
Hey presto! Beads are strung now and ready to make fast.

The love is in the sharing, as Molly wears her prize.
Their shine reflects the caring, the pride in Grandad's eyes.
A necklace made of conkers may not much value hold,
But yet, to those who made it, it's worth as much as gold!

– Maggie Ingall.

The Clocks

LATE summer has lost its brave battle with rain,
And days are much shorter, dark nights here again.
The nip in the air feels much keener and cold,
As the year now accepts it is soon growing old.

Leaves crispy, brown, red and gold, tumble from trees,
With joy dancing freely in each stirring breeze;
The greenhouse is cleared and plants safely indoors;
A squirrel is adding to his winter stores.

Much earlier in evenings the curtains are drawn,
Sometimes there's a frost, heavy dew on the lawn,
In cupboards warm coats and boots, gloves have been
found –
Though days can be sunny, a chill is around.

We welcome the thought of a warm, cosy fire,
Don't mind it's not summer, unwind and retire.
We let our thoughts follow an autumnal track,
Now we can accept that the clocks have gone back!

– Chrissy Greenslade.

from the Manse Window

Getting Away From It All

"LET'S take a boat to Bermuda, let's take a plane to St Paul . . . let's get away from it all."

That Sinatra evergreen classic! It's during the summer months that people generally take the opportunity to get away from it all, in order to refresh, recharge and regenerate themselves for the autumn and winter months ahead. Most of us at times feel the need to get away, and many regard the annual vacation as an absolute necessity!

Well, to get away was absolutely necessary for Jesus Christ at times, so how much more necessary must it be for we lesser mortals? Frequently in the New Testament we read of Jesus going off to a quiet place, either on his own or in the company of his disciples, to seek the peace and quiet which was so desperately needed, away from the pressures involved in the very unique vocation he had been given by God his Father.

In St Mark's Gospel, we read the account of Jesus being under unbelievable pressure while at the house of Simon and Andrew, due to the countless people coming to him for help and healing, far into the evening.

Thinkstockphotos.

"The whole city crowded together at the door," we are told and not one of them was turned away! But Jesus was physically exhausted, so early the next morning he rose and went to a quiet place to be with God his Father.

Jesus was well aware that if his unique, God-given mission meant that he was to be for ever giving out, he must at least on occasions be taking in!

LATER on in the same Gospel we read of the occasion when Jesus's disciples came back from a specific mission on which Jesus had sent them to report all they had done. They were tired and exhausted due to the pressure of the crowds, so much so that they hadn't even had time to eat!

Once again Jesus's strategy was to take them with him to a quiet and lonely spot across on the other bank of the lake, so that they might have some peace and rest for a short while.

Jesus knew that no-one could work without rest, and also that no-one could live the Christian life without making time for God.

God needs to be given the opportunity to speak to us, and we

By the Rev. Ian W.F. Hamilton.

in turn must take the opportunity and the time to be still and to listen to him. So once again Jesus – this time in the company of his disciples – decided to get away from it all.

PERHAPS one of the venues Jesus would often choose would be a garden. A garden is a good place in which to get away from it all!

I am reminded of the beautiful words written by the poet long-since:

"One is nearer God's heart in a garden than anywhere else on earth."

We delight in visiting the pleasant parks and gardens which beautify our green and pleasant country, and I'm certain many of you, like me, will have visited several gracious and splendid gardens abroad.

Perhaps this year, when you get away from it all, you will get the opportunity to visit some of the delightful gardens all around us!

On home ground, among the gardens I have visited and have much enjoyed are the famous Italian Gardens in Scarborough in Yorkshire, the Royal Botanical Gardens at Kew and, not least, the beautiful gardens which surround Brodie Castle in the Highlands of Scotland. I was privileged for so many years to have these gardens literally on my doorstep and we often escaped there in order to get away from it all!

Brodie Castle is especially famous for its wonderful and unique collection of daffodils, and in the springtime, when the grounds are absolutely carpeted with daffodils, the castle gardens are altogether breathtakingly beautiful!

It was the sight of a host of these lovely flowers that moved the poet William Wordsworth to pen his memorable words about wandering "lonely as a cloud, That floats on high o'er vales and hills."

Of course, Wordsworth wrote his lovely words at Grasmere in the north of England, but had he made a trip to the north of Scotland, and to Brodie Castle, he might have been moved to write his immortal words there, instead!

You, too, will have your favourite gardens to which you like to escape – gardens where, I am sure, the colour and variety and splendour you see will move your heart and soul to be "upward drawn to God".

It is always my experience that in the peace of a beautiful garden you are totally surrounded by the glory of God.

In the words of another poet, "What can we say, but 'Glory Be' when God breaks out in an apple tree!"

How true. The beauty of nature, the trees, the plants, the shrubs, the flowers; they all, in the words of one of my favourite hymns, "voiceless speak God's praise!"

SIGNIFICANTLY, towards the end of his earthly life it was to a garden that Jesus retired – the Garden of Gethsemane, situated high on the slopes of the Mount of Olives.

At this critical point in his life and mission Jesus retreated there to be near to his heavenly Father. It was an agonising time for Jesus, because it was in this garden that he had to come to terms with the excruciating pain and suffering that lay ahead of him.

It was in this garden that Jesus fell on his face in prayer and cried aloud, "My Father, if it be possible, let this cup pass from me, not as I will, but as you will."

It was in this garden that the loneliness of Jesus was all too evident, but it was also here, in Gethsemane, that his unshakable courage shone gloriously through.

Not least, it was in this garden that for Jesus Christ, the Son of God, "the shadow of a cross arose upon a lonely hill".

Yet, despite everything, it was here in this quiet quarter of retreat that Jesus felt especially close to God. It was in the Garden of Gethsemane that he prayerfully sought the strength for all the imminent pain and agony that clearly lay ahead of him.

I am perfectly sure that this is true for every one of us, namely that in the peace and quietness of a garden we can feel close to the God of creation, and seek his strength for all that the days and months and years ahead may bring to us.

So, wherever your holiday travels may take you as you get away from it all this year, and whether or not you have the chance to visit some lovely gardens, be sure that the God who said "I am with you always" will travel alongside you.

May you ever feel his gracious and loving presence close to you wherever you journey, so that you may return refreshed, revitalised, recharged and renewed! ■

Thinkstockphotos.

A Country Calendar For Autumn

■ Legend has it that, one night in the Middle Ages, all the men of Hinton St George went off to the fair. When they failed to return in the evening, the women of the village went looking for them by the light of candles inside pumpkins, or "punkies", as they called them.

This Somerset tradition continues on the last Thursday in October to this day, with children carving pumpkins and placing candles inside them, then marching through the streets with them.

■ If you have a nesting box for birds in your garden that has been used over the summer, now is the perfect time to give it a clean. Clear it out so that next year's families can use it – it'll also help prevent any potentially dangerous parasites finding a home in there for the winter.

If ducks do slide at Hallowtide, At Christmas they will swim; If ducks do swim at Hallowtide, at Christmas they will slide.

Thinkstockphotos.

■ Why not head out into the country and go blackberrying? Blackberries are still abundant in Britain, and as popular with the local wildlife as they are with us!

■ Grab your baskets and head into the woods for a spot of mushroom hunting. There are lots of organisations now running "fungi forays", so you can pick away without the fear of harvesting something that mightn't agree with you! Mushrooms are surrounded in folklore, as illustrated by their many fabulous names such as "Shaggy Inkcap", "Stinkhorn", "Slippery Jack" and "Saffron Milkcap".

FACT

A fresh autumn dew does wonders to bring out all the spiders' webs around and about. These beautiful, lightweight constructions are miracles of nature – on a weight-to-strength basis the silk from which they are made is five times the strength of steel, and can stretch between 35 and 40% without breaking. Spiders use them to catch prey, as their vision isn't good enough to go after their food in a more direct fashion!

■ As the year turns to autumn and first frosts begin, some hardy vegetables start to come into their own. A touch of frost seems to creat the sweetest parsnips, and the cabbages and sprouts are out in force. Apparently, sprouts are one of the nation's least-liked vegetable but a small handful of them fulfils most of your daily Vitamin C requirements!

Parsnips.

In Brambly Way

THROUGH coppice and bracken
We follow together
An old, mossy path on a fine, sunny day;
Where blackberries gleam
In the mild, autumn weather
And taste so much sweeter from Brambly Way!

With traveller's joy foaming
White floss on to hedgerows,
The robin still merrily piping away;
Small rabbits frisking
Around their home burrows,
Serene is the sunshine on Brambly Way.

When winter winds howl
And dark nights become chilly,
With window-panes frosting in awesome display,
We'll have warm, buttered toast
Spread with sweet bramble jelly –
Enjoying our harvest from Brambly Way!

– Maggie Smith.

Trick Or Treat

WHETHER it is trick or treat,
Hallowe'en is not complete
Without those little smiling faces,
Jumping out from hiding places.
Pointed hats and besom brushes,
Pumpkin lanterns hang from bushes,
And, with their witches' hats askew,
They trudge home for a barbecue:
Not slimy toads or slip'ry frogs,
But sizzling burgers and hot dogs!
So ends another Hallowe'en,
Fading now the magic scene.
To have again these times so dear,
We'll wait till witches fly next year . . .

– Brian H. Gent.

Remember, Remember

REMEMBER, remember the fifth of November.
How could we ever forget?
The smell of the smoke, the laughter and fun,
We store all the memories yet.
The magic of fireworks, heat of the fire,
The faces aglow with delight,
The sharing together with neighbours and friends
Excitement abroad in the night.

The children have waited so long for this day
So proudly displaying their guy,
Collecting the pennies and hoping for more,
The time seemed to go slowly by.
But now, as the fireworks light up the night
And shower their stars all about,
Amazement has captured their hearts and their minds
In wonder they laugh and they shout.

So often we all lose the magic of youth
Forgetting those times of delight,
But always remember the fifth of November
And the wonder of Bonfire Night!

– Iris Hesselden.

Fireworks

EAGER children gather round
With faces all aglow
In great anticipation
Of the forthcoming show.
For months they have been saving up,
Now, pocket money spent,
They're really looking forward to
This once-a-year event.

The whizzing, fizzing fireworks
Burst into sprays of light;
A shimmering of shining shapes
Start dancing in the night.
The rockets with their fiery tails
Go soaring way up high
And leave a trail of shooting stars
Across the inky sky.

As dazzling rainbows shower down
In glittering array,
A kaleidoscope of twinkling gems
Gives colourful display.
Roman candles, Catherine wheels
And sparklers burning bright
All add to the excitement of
This very special night.

– Kathleen Gillum.

The Memorial

THERE in stone, a granite cross
Tells us what our village lost.
At its foot are poppies red,
Which keep alive those heroes dead.
There's William Smith and Samuel John,
Now in a graveyard by the Somme,
And Peter Brown, who went to war
With the Royal Flying Corps,
And sixteen others we can see
Who died defending liberty.
Once they filled the school with noise,
Played football with the other boys;
Laughed and played, fished in the stream,
Chased the girls and ate ice-cream.
The mothers' grief and lovers' tears
Fulfilment of half-hidden fears.
And Jamie Green from Stanway Farm,
Killed on a road in Afghanistan,
They all lived here, this place their home,
We remember them still, their names in stone.

– ***Antony Burr.***

The Pleasure Of Reading

LEARNING to read is a wonderful thing,
As all through life it much pleasure can bring,
From tales of adventure which children adore,
To yarns about places we'd love to explore.

And tales of romance set in days long ago,
Or about modern folk like the ones that we know,
We feel for their problems, we hope they will find
A way to a future that's happy and kind.

And mysteries, too, hold us fast in their grip –
Will the villain escape in a cross-channel ship?
Or will the detective unravel the clues
And soon solve the crime that had made headline news?

We love all these stories, we're eager for more,
We love the adventures they bring to our door.
To sit and relax is our favourite thing,
Enjoying the pleasure that reading can bring.

– Rosemary Bennett.

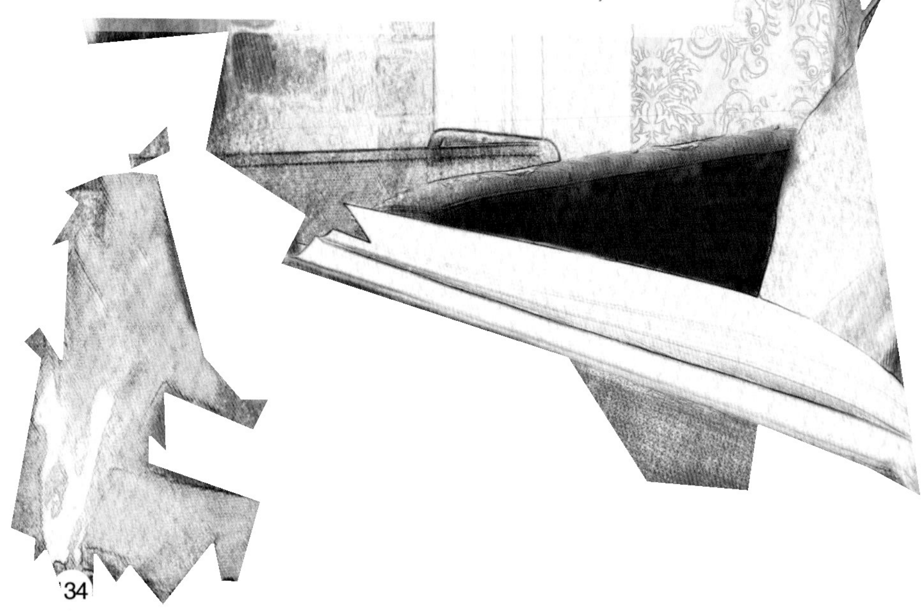

Place Of Peace

WE all need peaceful times to find
That place where cares are left behind,
A space where no-one can intrude
Into our treasure, solitude.

We all need laughter, company,
A time for great activity;
A time to talk and spread our wings –
But we can tire of all these things.

So rest a while, slow down your pace,
No matter where, you'll find a place,
On garden seat, beside the sea,
In parks and woodlands, peace is free.

Sitting at home in your armchair,
Just close your eyes and you'll find it there,
Go deep within and still your mind,
Tranquillity is there, you'll find.

Music can aid, uplift and heal,
And hidden depths within reveal,
As contentment then fills your soul,
You'll feel refreshed, you've reached your goal.

– Chrissy Greenslade.

Staying Warm

IT'S a crisp, clear day with a coverlet of snow,
So I'll pull on my boots and off walking I'll go.
"Don't you go out in the cold winter air.
Stay in by the fire. We've got cocoa to share!"
No, I'll pull on my coat, thick, warm and grey,
And I won't fear the chill on this cold winter day.
"Stay in! Stay in! It's cosy in here.
Stay close to the fire and join in our cheer."
No, I'll put on my scarf and wrap it around.
My neck will stay warm though there's snow on the ground.
"Don't step outside. There's a blanket of snow.
Be wrapped in my blanket. You don't have to go!"
No, I'll put on my hat to warm up my head.
I'd rather be walking than toasty in bed.
"Stay in! Stay warm! Buttered toast is the thing.
Who wants to go out before we see spring?"
No, I won't stay inside when snow shines in the sun,
And I won't just be walking, I'll skip and I'll run!
Stay warm? Oh, yes, I certainly will.
These fine winter woollies will keep out the chill!

– Antony Burr.

from the Manse Window

What A Privilege

THE taste of fizzy orange takes me back instantly to my childhood. I'm maybe nine or ten years old and am with the other children on the annual Sunday School Excursion.

We're sitting in our sandals and anoraks in a booth in one of those old-style seaside cafés in Portrush or Newcastle, looking out at the sea.

The drink is not in a big, refillable plastic thing like you get in Disneyland these days, but in a smaller, proper glass with a red straw. It's sweet, and the fizz gets up your nose, but you don't mind, for this is something of a rare treat.

I'm probably giving away my age here, but these were the days before huge supermarket chains, where you can now buy all manner of soft drinks in trays of a dozen or more.

We drank milk, mostly, in our house. There was a lemonade van that came round our way but I don't remember him ever stopping outside our house. I didn't discover coffee until my later teenage years. It seemed to arrive around the same time as peer pressure!

But with this fizzy memory come a flock of others from a happy, innocent childhood in Belfast. Slightly blurry pictures of the bread man, the coal man and Forth River Primary School. Wearing short trousers to the Boys' Brigade Junior Section in tall, grey, draughty church halls. Sitting beside Mum, drawing faces with my finger in the condensation on the window of the bus into town.

We didn't travel far, back then. This was long before I'd ever visited Egypt or Washington DC or climbed the Leaning Tower of Pisa.

Most of the sights and sounds and tastes of the world out there were still unknown to me. We saw pictures in books or maybe watched a cowboy film (in black and white, of course) on a Saturday afternoon, but that was about the height of it. I'd never been exposed to Chinese or Indian food. Pizza? What was that?

Our treat was vinegary chips and fizzy orange once a year in a seaside town, on a – usually chilly – day in June. But we didn't mind. We thought it was great.

I still remember the sense of adventure crossing the footbridge at Portballintrae, on the lookout for Indians in the sandhills, and becoming aware for the first time

Thinkstockphotos.

By the Rev. Andrew Watson.

of the immensity of the ocean as the waves came rolling and crashing in, massive, with surging white foam.

IT was more than enough for a young boy at the time, for I still had that sense of wonder. They say that familiarity breeds contempt, and that the more that is easily available to us, the less we appreciate. I think there's some truth here.

The world is now at our fingertips. We can travel every continent – literally or "virtually", seeing accurate colour satellite images of anywhere we want, and speaking face-to-face with friends or family in Australia via the internet.

There's usually any amount of fizzy drinks in the fridge, and the local supermarket stocks a wide range of exotic food from all over the place. We probably eat more international food now than traditional local cuisine!

I'm not complaining. I just don't want to take it for granted. I never want to lose my sense of wonder.

Perhaps that was one of the concerns of the writer of the New Testament book of Hebrews. Many of his readers were from a religious background, in which they had been taught they were safe and secure in God's loving providence. Weren't they God's favoured people? Hadn't he always kept his Covenant promises through the centuries to Abraham's descendants? Wouldn't he still provide, with the same compassion, patience and generosity as ever?

In one sense that is fair enough, but for some the temptation might be to take God's kindness for granted. For believers who were raised in a religious setting it could be easy to let their background knowledge of God and his grace, and their familiarity with the Good News of Jesus and his love, allow them to slip into a dismissive attitude, or just become complacent!

And so the writer goes to great lengths in this book to emphasise just how wonderful Jesus is. Much superior, for example, to Old Testament hero Moses, who had always been something of a national icon:

"Moses was faithful as a servant in all God's house, testifying to what would be said in the future. But Christ is faithful as a son over God's house." (Hebrews 3 v 5, 6)

Furthermore, Jesus was greater than the priests who served in the Temple bringing sacrifices to God on behalf of the people. They were human and flawed like the rest of us, and the offerings they made were imperfect. Jesus, however, was perfectly holy.

"We do not have a High Priest who is unable to sympathise with our weaknesses, but we have One who has been tempted in every way, just as we are – yet was without sin. Let us then approach the throne of grace with confidence, so that we may receive mercy . . . " (Hebrews 4 v 15, 16)

Christ is also presented as much superior to the angels. They were created but Jesus is God's eternal Son, without beginning or end, the Divine Mediator through whom we may approach the Almighty in His awesome holiness:

"The Son is the radiance of God's glory and the exact representation of His being, sustaining all things by His powerful word. After He had provided purification for sins, He sat down at the right hand of the Majesty in heaven. So He became as much superior to the angels as the name He has inherited is superior to theirs." (Hebrews 1 v 3,4)

So he was not just a good man, a gifted teacher or another healer. Jesus was absolutely unique and wonderful in the true sense of that word. The writer challenges us –

"We must pay more careful attention . . . so that we do not drift away . . . How shall we escape if we neglect such a great salvation?" (Hebrews 2 v 1-3)

Jesus is so wonderful and so necessary that we cannot afford to ignore him or to take him for granted!

Rather we should be offering our whole lives in obedient service to bring honour to such an amazing Lord, who has proved himself our gracious friend.

"What a friend we have in Jesus, all our sins and griefs to bear. What a privilege to carry everything to God in prayer!"

May we never cease to enjoy the colourful variety God gives all around us, the awesome forces in nature, the sights, vibrant colours and eclectic tastes from around the world.

More importantly, may we never cease to trust, obey and wonder in the awesome person and work and deep love of our Saviour! ■

Thinkstockphotos.

A Country Calendar For Winter

■ The Roman festival of Saturnalia began on December 17. What started off as a day's celebration soon became a week, and was presided over by a master of the revels. As many of the festival's customs became absorbed into British culture, that person became known in England as the Lord of Misrule and in Scotland as the Abbot of Unreason!

■ Some say that a proper Christmas pudding should contain 13 ingredients to represent Jesus and his Disciples, and that every member of the family should have a go at stirring the mix – in an east to west direction, in honour of the pilgrimage of the Wise Men.

If Christmas day be bright and clear,
There'll be two winters in the year.

Northern lights, USA.

■ With the long, dark nights, some of us may be lucky enough to see the Northern Lights – or indeed the Southern Lights. Although it's generally considered that you have to be far north or far south to see them, the Great Geomagnetic Storm in 1859 produced auroras so significant that large portions of the world were able to see them. In fact, the New York Times reported that in Boston one Friday, the aurora was "so brilliant that at about one o'clock in the morning, ordinary print could be read by the light."

There's a bit of folklore which says that all animals can speak on Christmas Eve. Unfortunately, it's bad luck actually to test this superstition!

A light dusting of snow gives the perfect opportunity to practise your animal tracking – a simple country walk can become a detective hunt!

WildStock.

Keep an eye out for the elegant double grooves of the deer, the clustered dents of a running rabbit or even a badger track with its deep claw marks and five digits, if you're lucky!

FACT

At this time of year, mistletoe is often used as a good excuse for a stolen kiss. Unfortunately, it can't really be used for a lot else by us humans, as it is toxic if digested. However, the berries and leaves are a fantastic, high-protein food for many animals, including our precious bees.

Although recent years in Britain have seen some substantial falls of snow, spare a thought for our American and Canadian friends who have ice storms to contend with!

An ice storm is when precipitation falls warm enough to be rain or sleet, then freezes as it enters a cold layer of air near the ground, instantly coating whatever it touches in a layer of ice.

Ice storms have brought down branches, trees, power lines and even pylons due to the weight of the encrusted ice!

Frozen in motion.

Swirling Visions

SNOWFLAKES drifting all around me,
Banners of ethereal grace,
Borne upon the winds of midnight,
Gathered to their resting place.
Silently in swirling visions,
Teeming from each sculptured cloud,
Weaving wonders with their patterns,
Milling as a jostling cloud.
Snowflakes spread across the landscape,
Picturesque for all to see,
Giving us a glimpse of nature's
Dazzling winter scenery.

– Elizabeth Gozney.

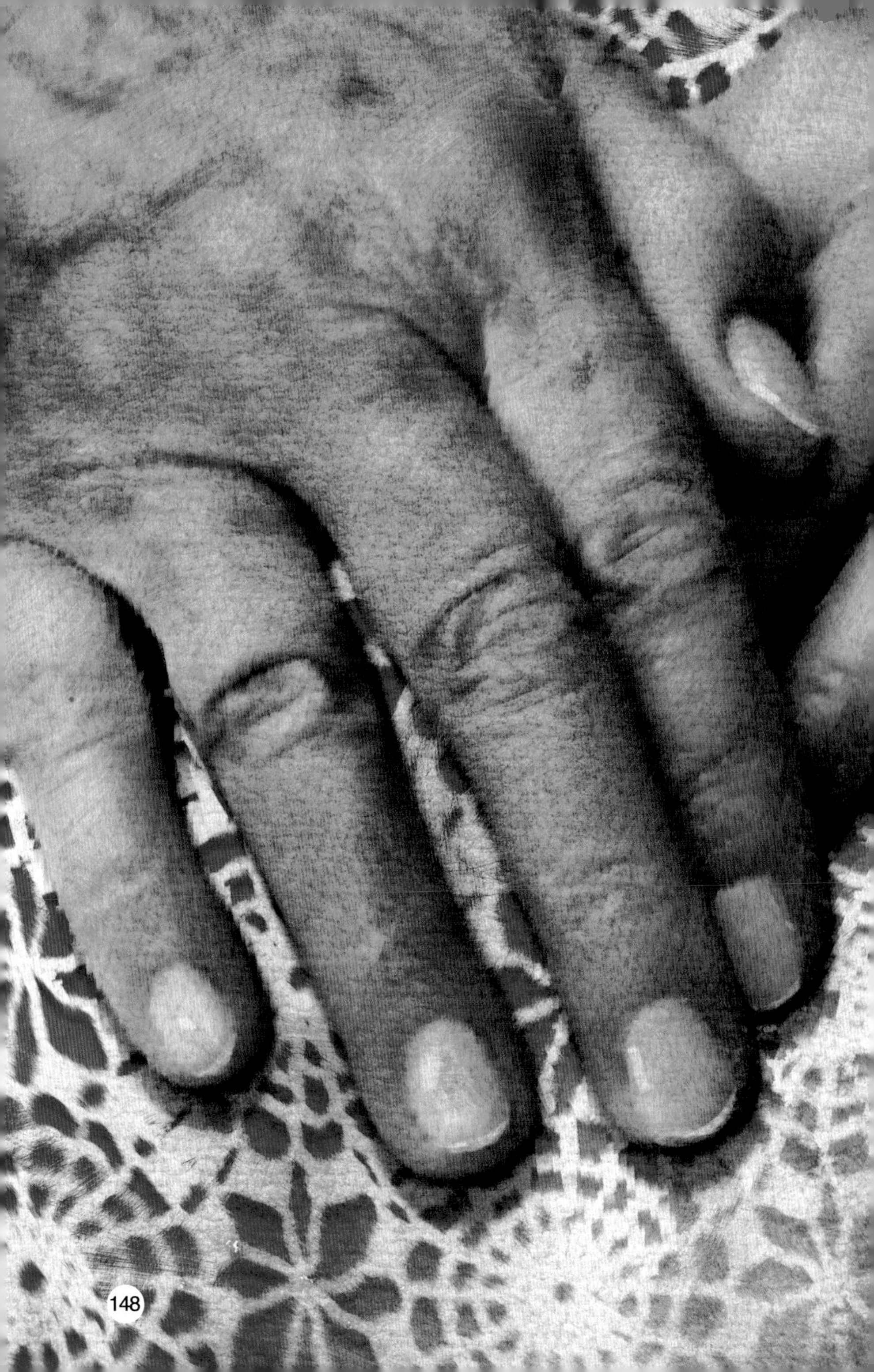

Hands

ONCE elegant, slim, but now not so,
Nails long and painted to match my toe,
Hands that express emotion while talking
And sway to and fro when out walking.

Once showed off the diamond ring,
The day it came, how my heart did sing!
E'en more so when encircled in gold,
Promising to honour and obey till old.

Now the finger holds a third ring,
Once worn by him who made my heart sing,
The last time together, these hands caressed,
Before he left me and our life blessed.

Hands that worked hard around the home,
Bringing up children till their time to roam,
Still able and busy with cooking and baking,
Though sometimes on days found tired and aching.

Wrinkled and broader, what stories to tell,
Of seventy-four years, used so well,
Holding, handling, touching and caressing,
In a life which has received much blessing.

– Helen Currie.

Snuggle Down

WHEN winter comes with icy winds,
And storms of snow and sleet,
We long to settle before the fire
In a cosy, snug retreat.

Or to snuggle down in our nice warm bed
Until eight o'clock or nine,
And not to get up and go outdoors
Till the sun begins to shine.

But though the days are short and cold,
When winter comes each year,
Not all the things that winter brings
Are always dull and drear.

For there's Christmastime and Hogmanay,
With their joy and friendship, too,
And on frosty days the countryside
Delights our gaze anew.

So when winter comes, though nights are long,
There are pleasures to be found,
And if we wrap up to face the cold,
We shall find them all around.

– ***Rosemary Bennett.***

The Thought That Counts

THE market had seemed like a place from my dreams,
With lanterns that shone in the snow,
And I had it in mind that I wanted to find
A present for my auntie Flo.

There were stalls that sold food that smelled very good,
With their *Bratwurst* and *Glühwein* and such,
And iced ginger cakes like a *Hausfrau* might make,
Which I always enjoy very much.

I found angels and stars and toy trains and cars,
And a life-sized nativity set,
And a reindeer that glowed when you patted his nose,
Which Aunt Flo would have hated, I bet.

Now the crowd was so thick I could have done with a stick
To fight my way through to each stall,
But each time I got there, much to my despair,
For Aunt Flo I found nothing at all.

It seemed to me rash to spend loads of cash
On a present that wasn't quite right,
But after hours on the go and still nothing to show,
I might end up looking all night.

She wouldn't want socks or a cup filled with chocs,
Or a ball that lit up with each bounce.
Then I suddenly thought that, whatever I bought,
It's the love that goes with it that counts.

– Antony Burr.

The Children's Carol Service

THE Head had decided that all of the tinies
Would sit in a group near the huge Christmas tree,
Which stood in its glory just by the main staircase;
The rest of the choir waiting there patiently.

The parents and grandparents gathered together
All eager to see where their own child might be,
And when they were spotted, such beams of excitement!
"Oh, look! There's our Jack! Over there – can't you see?"

The carols then started, the young voices soaring
And rising up high to the tree's shining star;
They told us of angels, a stable, a baby,
And wise men who came from a land afar.

Then stood up the tinies – their moment of glory!
All combed, scrubbed and shining, their eyes round and bright;
So earnest they stood there and sang their small hearts out,
Their faces reflecting the tree's starry light.

And as their sweet voices tugged all of our heartstrings,
There suddenly came from the darkness above
A sprinkling of snowflakes, all sparkling and spinning,
To frost children singing of peace and of love.

I felt my eyes prickling – I just couldn't help it –
And slipped out a hankie to hide every trace.
I needn't have worried as, glancing around me,
I saw teardrops glistening on every proud face.

– Eileen Hay.

Inner Beauty

LOOK at life through eyes of love,
And see the world anew
By dwelling on the beautiful,
What's good and pure and true.
Let ideas into your mind,
Be filled with precious things –
Inspiring and uplifting thoughts
And hopes that soar on wings.

Enthusiasm, courage, joy,
With cheerfulness and grace,
Radiating from within,
Will show upon your face.
Cultivate a happy heart,
Compassionate and kind,
For beauty in your spirit is
Reflected in your mind.

– Kathleen Gillum.

Christmas Robins

On Christmas cards and calendars
These merry birds abound;
Our Christmas robins bring us cheer
Wherever they are found.

We love their vivid colouring,
Their bold and fearless gaze,
Their friendliness to humans
And their cute, amusing ways.

They add a touch of gaiety
On days so dark and drear,
Our little Christmas robins
With their message of good cheer.

– Rosemary Bennett.

from the Manse Window

Warmth And Light

AUTUMN was the time for open fires in the vicarage grate. They made the sitting-room glow with warmth and light. As children we found them a great comfort. You could sit near the fire when the wind was howling outside and watch the sparks flying up the chimney.

It was one of the few times when we felt warm. There was no central-heating back in the Forties!

We liked them for another reason. The house was Victorian, full of dark passageways, cellars, attics and unexpected corners. In those days there was no electricity and we relied on oil lamps, which threw shadows everywhere. We did have night lights burning when we went to bed, but they did little to banish the gloom. A roaring fire drove away all the ghosts good and proper!

Each wood had a different smell. Pine was a favourite. It burned with a sharp, resinous scent and made a crackling noise, every so often bursting out into a cascade of sparks.

Oak was rich and fruity, which is why it is used for smoking some cheeses and fish. Apple, cherry, pear and plum burn with a wonderful scent, but they are hard to come by, except when you have to lop off a dead branch. Nobody wants to cut down trees that are bearing a good crop of fruit!

Some wood burns better than others. Elder is smoky, and elm smoulders without throwing out a great deal of heat. Spruce needs to be treated with care as it burns like fury and gives sparks in all directions.

My favourite is ash. It produces great heat and plenty of flame and best of all it is one of the few woods that goes well when it is green.

IN the early days of my ministry we lived on a tight budget and could not always afford lorry-loads of logs. The vicarage was surrounded by woods so we used to have Saturday morning wood-gathering expeditions, taking along a crosscut saw and wheelbarrow.

There were always plenty of fallen branches to cut up and the owner was glad to have the timber cleared away. You ended up with stiff shoulders from so much sawing, but it was worth it in the end because it meant a nice blazing fire for the evening.

By the Rev. David Bryant.

God has often been described in terms of fire down the ages. When Moses was looking after a flock of sheep for his father-in-law, he had a vision of God in the form of a burning bush in the desert.

"And the angel of the Lord appeared to him in a flame of fire out of the midst of a bush; and he looked and lo, the bush was burning, yet it was not consumed."

The prophet Ezekiel, who comforted the Hebrew people when they were exiled to Babylon, describes his calling.

"As I looked, behold a stormy wind came out of the north, and a great cloud with brightness round about it, and the fire, flashing forth continually and in the midst of the fire, as it were, gleaming bronze."

There is a story in St John's Gospel that links together Jesus and fire. The disciples have been out fishing all night, and when they bring the boat in to the shore they are surprised to find a charcoal fire burning on the sand. They go closer and find that he is busy cooking fish over the embers.

"Come and have breakfast," he tells them.

Then he passes bread and fish to them and they know that he has truly risen.

ONE of the most familiar sights and smells of autumn is the bonfire. There is nothing better when you are digging the garden on a cold day. You can stand close and get warmed up, and at the same time throw on all the unwanted weeds and rubbish.

I remember peeking through Father's study window when he was writing a sermon, longing for him to finish so that he could come into the garden and set light to the bonfire that lay waiting.

Often we cadged a few potatoes off our mother and put them in the red-hot ashes. We fished them out a couple of hours later and ate them. Nothing ever tasted so delicious as those charred, black, half-cooked King Edwards.

When I look back over the years, I can recall many instances of fire that have reminded me of the reassuring presence of God.

In our village after the war we had a night watchman. He had a little hut and in front of it was a burning brazier to keep him warm during the small hours. His job was to warn people of trenches and holes where the road had been dug up. Sometimes, if we were lucky, he would give us chestnuts that he had roasted on the embers, and he never minded if we paused to warm our hands on a snowy night.

Then there was the huge bonfire on VE Day, which the whole village attended. The men threw on a few barrels of tar to add to the celebrations and there was a wonderful feeling in the air. Peace had come again. More recently, there were beacons lit all over the world in a thousand places to celebrate the Diamond Jubilee of the Queen.

Many holy men and women have chosen to speak of God as fire. Hildegard of Bingen, a nun living in the 12th century, wrote this –

"It is easier to gaze into the sun than into the face of the mystery of

God. Such is its beauty and radiance."

Richard Rolle, a Yorkshire hermit living a century later, wrote a book about God. He called it, "The Fire Of Love." Many Bible passages use similar language. On the day of Pentecost the coming of the Holy Spirit is described as being like tongues of fire.

From very earliest times mankind has valued fire. It gives us warmth when the weather is cold and the dark and the autumn nights are closing in. It provides comfort and hope when we are feeling under the weather. It throws light into the "unlovely" places of the world, banishing the darkness, and it is always a welcome sight to see logs burning brightly on the hearth. Fire is a reminder of the presence of God all around us.

One of Charles Wesley's most moving hymns speaks of God as fire.

"O thou who camest from above, the pure celestial fire to impart,

Kindle a flame of sacred love, upon the mean altar of my heart.

There let it for thy glory burn, with inextinguishable blaze,

And trembling to its source return, in humble prayer and fervent praise."

I can think of no better prayer for autumn than these beautiful lines. ■

Thinkstockphotos.

A Country Calendar For Winter

■ Up Helly Aa is the larg…

■ Brightening up the dark mid-January evenings is Burns Night. Every January 25, Scots all over the world gather to celebrate arguably their greatest poet with a traditional meal of haggis, neeps and tatties. Don't forget to stand when the main course is brought in!

■ In the Little Ice Age between 1550 and 1750, the climate was so cold that even the Thames froze over every year. Sometimes this great freeze would last for over three months! Enterprising Londoners set up a Frost Fair on the river, with tents, sideshows and ice sports.

The last Frost Fair was held in 1814, when an elephant was led across the river below Blackfriars Bridge.

Thinkstockphotos.

To read a poem in January is as lovely as to go for a walk in June.
– Jean-Paul Sartre.

Make the most of the season's leeks, a classic northern European vegetable and a relative of garlic and onions. The smaller leeks tend to be sweet and more tender – better for quicker cooking or side dishes – but whatever size, make sure you give them a thorough wash!

The Anglo-Saxons used to call the first month of their year "Wolf monath". Being in the midst of winter meant that the increasingly hungry wolves would be starting to come down to the villages in search of food.

FACT

It's tempting to think that Boxing Day might be named after the big job of clearing up after Christmas, but it stems from the tradition of employers giving a gift, or "Christmas box", to their servants or tradespeople on this day.

The gift of giving.

The Christmas Card

THE scene upon the Christmas card
Depicts a time that's flown,
When life was not so hectic
And commercial as our own.
When simple pleasures brought delight,
And folk made time to greet,
With friendly words and cheery smiles,
Their neighbours in the street.

And if we find a little time
To do these simple things,
We'll spread more friendliness around,
And all the joy it brings.
Then, like the friendly days of old,
There'll be real Christmas cheer,
And kindness and companionship
Will last through all the year.

– Rosemary Bennett.

If Only

OUTSIDE it's dark, and yet I know
That morning's almost here,
For daylight dawns reluctantly
This dismal time of year.
I hear the rain upon the pane,
I hear the cold winds storm;
I snuggle down beneath my sheets,
So glad I'm safe and warm.
I know I have some minutes more
Before I need to rise,
So, till I do, I'll just lie still
And briefly close my eyes.
Oh, how I wish we humans had
Evolved a different way,
What bliss 'twould be to hibernate,
And not get up till May!

– ***Maggie Ingall.***

The Sales

THE turkey has been eaten,
The washing-up all done,
The presents are all put aside
With thanks to everyone.
But now it's time for winter sales,
It's Boxing Day once more,
There may be bargains to be found
In every busy store.

The traffic will be hectic
As people flock to town,
But never mind, excitement reigns
As we rush up and down.
We look at this and look at that,
There's "buy one, get one free",
And then we need to take a rest
And have a cup of tea.

Then, still a little weary,
For now it's getting late,
We're on our way with lots of bags.
This Boxing Day was great!

– *Iris Hesselden.*

If At First You Don't Succeed

IT really is a misconception,
Yet each year we do the same.
Most of us without exception
Make resolutions once again.

At the start of each New Year
We list things we'll strive to achieve.
We'll contact friends both far and near
And keep faith in all that we believe.

On looking back, which resolutions
Made this year now still hold strong?
If not all, there's one solution –
Try again, when this year's gone!

– Joan Zambelli.

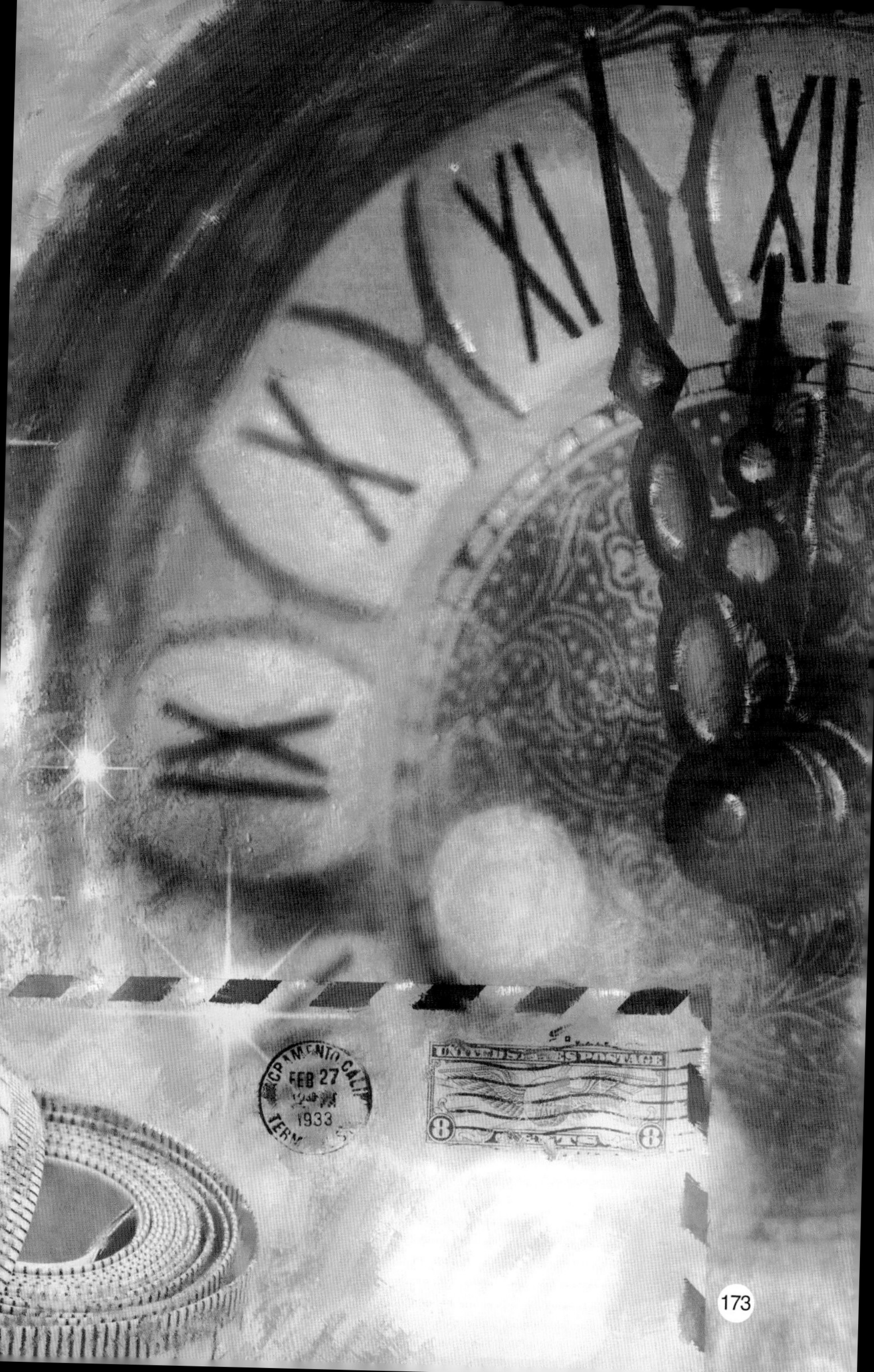
XII
XI
X
IX
FEB 27
1933
POSTAGE
8
8

My heart's in the Highlands,
my heart is not here;
My heart's in the Highlands,
chasing the deer.

– Robert Burns.